PATHFINDER'S JOURNEY

SHIVKUMAR RAI

With heartfelt gratitude, this book is dedicated to my fellow trekkers whose companionship and support were invaluable during our trek. A special thanks also goes to those who inspired me to pen down the tales of our adventure.

Contents

Acknowledgements — *vii*

About the Author — *ix*

Preface — *xi*

Blob / Book Summary — *xiii*

1. From Novice To Finisher: My First Half Marathon Tale — 1

2. Scaling Heights: Our Mountain Odyssey — 7

3. Three Musketeers' Himalayan Odyssey — 16

4. Conquering Mount Ophir's Heights — 23

5. Mountain Echoes: Trials And Triumphs On Mount Belumut — 28

6. Peak Pursuits: Tales Of 5 Trek — 35

7. A Day To Remember — 39

8. Trek To Kota Tinggi — 42

9. Stair Climbing Challenge — 47

10. Conquering Singapore's Round Island Route: A Month-Long Adventure — 50

11. Strides Together: Building Fitness And Community With Fun4walk — 55

12. A Century Ride To Remember — 58

Acknowledgements

Big thanks to Rohit Jaiswal and Ashish Mishra for helping me through my first half-marathon.

I'm really grateful to Arvind Joshi, Hemant, Bhushan, and Sadhu bhai for joining me on the Pangarchula trek. They were the reason I went on my first trip, and I had a great time.

A shoutout to Arvind Tiwari and Vikram Awasthi for being with me on the Kedarkantha hike. The story in 'A Story of Three Musketeers in the Himalayas' wouldn't be complete without them.

Thanks to Manish S, Amit Giri, and Vivek Singh for their company on the C2C trip. It was a beautiful experience.

I'm thankful to Manoj Pandey for joining the 150km RIR trek. He's a good friend and always ready to join in.

Special thanks to Sanjay, Pritesh Shah, and Mamta Deshmukh for their big help in my sports journey. We started as trekking buddies and became good friends.

Thanks to Gajanand for leading the 100km cycle rise and encouraging us. He's a simple guy with great skills.

Thank you to all my trekking friends who always come along on hikes.

Thanks to my son Siddharth Rai for his great help with proofreading.

Last but not least, a huge thank you to my wife, Archana, for always pushing me to do my best. This book wouldn't be here without her.

About The Author

Shivkumar Rai, a passionate technologist, has a deep-rooted love for learning and research. His journey began in the quaint village of Palhaiya, located in the Bhadohi district of Uttar Pradesh, where he spent his formative years.

His academic pursuits led him to the SP Jain School of Global Management in Singapore, where he completed an executive MBA in finance in 2014. Adding to his impressive credentials, he also participated in the Entrepreneurs Surge program at the Indian Institute of Management, Kolkata, in 2022.

A sports enthusiast at heart, he relishes engaging in activities like hiking, cricket, and tennis. Additionally, he finds joy in creating stories inspired by his personal sporting adventures.

ABOUT THE AUTHOR

Shivkumar beams with pride as the father of three wonderful kids and currently resides in Singapore with his family.

• x •

Preface

This book is a story of my own sports experience—a journey that began as a personal endeavour, never intended for the eyes beyond my own. I confess, the prospect of sharing these tales with the outside world fills me with a mixture of nervous excitement and humble gratitude. It's a leap into unfamiliar terrain, as writing has been my solace—a means to pen down my experiences, to weave tales that found their way onto the digital canvas of LinkedIn.

What started as a collection of short stories shared online, capturing the essence of my sporting escapades, has now found a home within the pages of this book. The transition from personal hobby to published work feels both surreal and exhilarating.

With every chapter meticulously crafted, I've strived to encapsulate not just my victories and challenges but also the lessons learned along the way. Each tale holds within it a nugget of wisdom gleaned from the trails, the races, and the camaraderie forged amidst sweat and determination.

As I share these stories—each a mosaic of personal growth and shared experiences—I hope to offer not just glimpses into my world but also insights that transcend the boundaries of sport. It's an attempt to distil the lessons learned from the track, the mountain, and the shared pursuit of the extraordinary.

So, as these narratives unfold, I invite you to embark on this journey with me. Let these stories not just be about sports but about the beauty of resilience, the power of community, and the remarkable transformations that occur when passion meets the written word.

Blob / Book Summary

Pathfinder's Journey is an inspiring memoir by Shivkumar Rai. In this captivating book, Rai shares his exhilarating experiences in sports and trekking. Each chapter unfolds a different adventure, from grueling marathons to challenging mountain expeditions, offering readers a glimpse into the demanding yet rewarding world of extreme physical challenges. Rai's personal journey is not just about physical endurance; it's a testament to the power of resilience, self-discovery, and the profound lessons learned from nature and perseverance. This book is a must-read for adventure enthusiasts and anyone seeking inspiration to overcome life's hurdles.

CHAPTER ONE

From Novice to Finisher: My First Half Marathon Tale

In the beginning, there was a man, a battle, and a run so legendary it would kick off one of the most exhausting yet exhilarating human activities known to modern sneakers: the marathon. Picture this: 490 BCE, Greece. Our hero, Pheidippides, sprints from the battlefield of Marathon to Athens with a joyous spoiler alert: "We won!" Then, as if to say, "My job here is done," he promptly drops dead. Now, if that's not commitment to delivering good news, I don't know what is.

Fast forward a few millennia, and someone thought, "Hey, why not commemorate this epic sprint of yore with a race of our own?" And so, at the rebirth of the Olympics in 1896, in Athens no less, the marathon made its modern debut. They roughly retraced our ancient postman's steps, give or take a few miles for dramatic effect, igniting what would become the global marathon mania.

But it was the 1908 London Olympics that truly put the marathon on the map, or rather, decided its exact mileage. In a move that would make any GPS envious, they stretched the race to finish in front of royal eyes, clocking in at precisely 26 miles and 385 yards. This distance, seemingly plucked from the sky (or rather, the royal whims), became the gold standard for marathons worldwide. Because, as we all know, nothing says "sporting precision" like rounding up to the nearest yard for royalty.

Since then, the marathon has exploded from an elite footrace to a global block party on the run, where thousands of brave (or perhaps delusional) souls from all walks of life lace up their running shoes to chase glory, personal bests, or at the very least, a really good story and a free banana at the finish line. Cities around the globe now host these 26.2-mile parties, from Boston to Berlin, where the streets are lined not with cheering spectators but with fellow sufferers in solidarity, all thinking, "Whose bright idea was this, anyway?"

And let's not forget the women who crashed the marathon boys' club. Take Kathrine Switzer, who in 1967 snuck into the Boston Marathon disguised with a number and a dream, outrunning prejudice to pave the way for future generations of women proving, once and for all, that endurance knows no gender.

This book, dear reader, is not just the recounting of a person's journey through the highs, lows, and cramps of running a marathon. It's an ode to the human spirit, a tale of ordinary people doing something extraordinary: waking up ridiculously early, pounding the pavement, and pushing their limits, all in the pursuit of that elusive finish line. So, strap on your running shoes (or open a bag of chips, no judgment here), and let's dive into a story that celebrates not just the physical marathon, but the marathon of life itself. Buckle up; it's going to be a bumpy ride.

On that memorable day, the 29th of May 2016, I etched my name into the pages of my personal history, and the OSIM SUNDOWN MARATHON, 2016, became more than just a race; it evolved into a profound life lesson.

The fascination of a half marathon, which is exactly half the distance of a standard marathon, has always intrigued me. I was aware that it represented a physical and mental challenge of a different order, and the OSIM SUNDOWN MARATHON, renowned as the largest mass night run in Singapore, provided the ideal stage for this ambition.

But the path to that day was marked by an unwavering commitment to hard work and dedication. My journey officially commenced in December 2015, when I resolved to participate in a half marathon. As a newcomer to the world of long-distance running, I understood the importance of a meticulous and structured approach to my training.

My initial foray into training involved daily 3-kilometre walks performed five days a week. It may have seemed modest, but it served as the foundation for my later endeavours. Those early morning walks were more than just physical exercise; they were a ritual that reinforced my determination. They instilled in me a sense of commitment and a daily reminder of my ultimate goal.

During those initial two months, my focus was on building stamina and acclimatizing my body to the rigours of walking over extended distances. The foundation was established, and it was time to gradually intensify my training.

The turning point in my journey happened on the 20th of February 2016 when I participated in the Marina Run, a challenging 10-kilometer race. It was a day filled with both excitement and anxiety, a mix of emotions that would become familiar to me as I continued my journey. For this race, I adopted a strategy that combined walking and running to optimize my energy levels. Crossing that finish line was more than just a physical achievement; it was a testament to my evolving determination and the effectiveness of my training program.

The sense of accomplishment that enveloped me after completing the Marina Run was electrifying. It was not merely about the distance I had covered, but the realization that my goal was within reach. That success provided the impetus to elevate my training regimen, transitioning to a 5-kilometer distance, five days a week. The mix of walking and running became my hallmark, a model that challenged my limits while keeping the training enjoyable.

Another significant milestone in my journey was the JP Morgan Corporate Challenge on the 28th of April 2016. This race, spanning 5.6 kilometres, was not only an opportunity to push my boundaries but also to gauge my progress. To my delight, I completed this race even faster than the previous one. The feeling of progress was invigorating, reinforcing my belief that my training regimen was indeed on the right track.

But the most awaited moment was still on the horizon, the OSIM SUNDOWN MARATHON, a race that would test my limits like never before. I had envisioned this day with a mix of excitement and nervous anticipation, a moment that would serve as the culmination of months of dedication and unwavering commitment.

As the event date drew nearer, the buzz in the running community about the OSIM SUNDOWN MARATHON was palpable. It wasn't just a race; it was an experience, a collective journey of individuals who, like me, were pursuing personal goals.

The night of the marathon was a spectacle to behold. The city of Singapore, under the cover of a starry night, was transformed into a realm of determination and endurance. As I joined thousands of other runners at the starting line, the atmosphere was electric. The collective energy was both exhilarating and intimidating.

The course, though daunting, offered a unique perspective of the city's landscape. Running through the heart of Singapore, I witnessed the city come to life in the early morning hours. The illuminated streets and cheering spectators were a testament to the spirit of the event. With each step, I inched closer to my goal.

The 21.1 kilometres felt like a formidable distance, but I was prepared. The key, I had learned during my training, was to maintain a steady pace, one that allowed me to conserve energy for the later stages of the race. The presence of fellow runners, each with their own stories and motivations, was inspiring. It was a reminder that I was part of a larger community, one that celebrated both individual achievements and collective spirit.

As the finish line approached, a surge of emotions washed over me. It wasn't just about physical endurance; it was a testament to the human spirit's resilience. Crossing that finish line was more than a personal victory; it was a celebration of discipline, perseverance, and the unwavering commitment to a goal. The sense of achievement was profound.

The lessons I took away from this journey were not limited to running. They transcended the realm of sports and entered the realm of life itself. I realized that every goal, no matter how distant it may seem, begins with a resolute mindset. It's about making that initial commitment and following it up with dedicated practice.

The journey to a half marathon mirrored life's challenges. It taught me that, like in running, life's most significant accomplishments require consistent effort, patience, and the belief that with each step, we come closer to our goals. It was a lesson in determination, discipline, and the power of a resilient spirit.

Looking back, that half marathon was more than just a race; it was a journey of self-discovery. It was a testament to the power of resilience and the unwavering human spirit. It reinforced the belief that, no matter how daunting a challenge may seem, the journey to success begins with a single step, guided by a resolute mind and an unwavering spirit to keep moving forward.

The OSIM SUNDOWN MARATHON, 2016, was a significant chapter in my life. It marked the beginning of a new phase, one where self-belief and commitment would shape my approach to life's challenges. This experience was a reminder that the journey itself is as valuable as the destination, and with the right mindset, no goal is too distant to achieve.

CHAPTER TWO

Scaling Heights: Our Mountain Odyssey

"Climb the mountains, not so the world can see you, but so you can see the world!"

Mountains have long stood as powerful symbols in the human psyche, embodying the ultimate test of endurance, the pinnacle of achievement, and the solitude necessary for introspection and personal growth. They represent not just physical but also metaphorical peaks, challenging us to rise above our limitations and offering profound lessons on perseverance, humility, and the pursuit of excellence. In the narrative of life, mountains are the silent witnesses to our most pivotal moments, encouraging us to push forward, even when the path seems insurmountable.

The mountain, with its harsh weather, treacherous paths, and breath-taking vistas, serves as the perfect backdrop for this journey of self-discovery. The physical challenges of the trek—navigating rocky trails, enduring the cold, battling fatigue—parallel the emotional and psychological trials the protagonist faces. With every obstacle overcome on the mountain, a layer of self-doubt is stripped away, revealing a stronger, more resilient self.

The seeds of our incredible journey were sown in early 2017 when some of my colleagues yearned for an adventurous escape from the confines of Singapore. Our research and wanderlust led us to a unanimous decision - the mountains beckoned. Excitement coursed through our veins. When the notion of hiking in the pristine realm of Uttarakhand was put forward, I was the first to leap at the opportunity.

With a resounding "Let's get going!!", our course was set.

We meticulously planned a 9-day odyssey, a tapestry of destinations including Deoriatal, Chandrashila summit, Chopta, Auli, Kuari Pass, and the formidable Pangarchula Summit. We set about honing our physical and mental prowess for this expedition with two months of gruelling preparation - running, walking, cycling - all building towards this crescendo. A week before our trek commenced, we initiated a dialogue with our trek staff, who would soon become our trail companions.

The day of reckoning was upon us. Four of us, Arvind, Hemant, Bhushan, and I, touched down in Delhi, India, the gateway to Devbhoomi, the 'Land of the Gods.'

Day 1 - Rishikesh – Sari-Deoriatal

Our inaugural day began at 5:30 AM, as we embarked on a road trip from Rishikesh to a village named Sari. Along the journey, the majestic Ganges River flowed to our right, while the towering mountains graced our left. It was an invigorating start to our adventure. Eight hours later, we arrived in Sari, where we were greeted by our Trek Leaders, guide, and technical instructor - an impressive and enthusiastic ensemble.

After exchanging pleasantries, we commenced our ascent towards Deoriatal, a 2.5 km trek from Sari. Despite the weariness from the long journey, every step through the enchanting forest trails was a symphony of nature's finest. We spent the night by the pristine lake at Deoriatal, basking in the moon's gentle reflections, and awoke the next morning to the ethereal sight of the snow-clad Chaukhamba peak. Chaukhamba holds immense spiritual significance for Hindus, as it is believed to be one of the places where Lord Shiva performed his meditation. The connection to the source of the Ganges River, which is considered holy by millions, adds to the aura of this place.

Day 2 unfolded as a long and arduous hike that started with a hearty breakfast. Setting out for Chopta via Rohini Bugyal, renowned for its lush meadows, the air was crisp, our spirits soaring, and the ambience serenely tranquil. Over nine hours, we covered 18 km and reached an elevation of 8790 feet. This route offered a diverse spectrum of experiences, from forested paths to verdant fields and challenging rocky terrains. It's a journey that words alone cannot truly convey.

Upon our arrival in Chopta, often dubbed the 'mini-Switzerland of Uttarakhand,' we discovered our tents nestled in an expansive green field. After a scrumptious dinner, we retired to our sleeping bags under the starry embrace.

"There is no Wi-Fi in the forest, but I promise you'll find a better connection."

We took a day to rest in the Chopta camp, welcoming the arrival of our colleague, Saju Bhai. Our Trek Leader, Montu Bhai, delineated the plan for our next challenge - the Chandrashila Summit. Our alarms were set for a daunting 02:30 AM wake-up call.

Day 3 – Chopta - Tungnath – Chandrashila

At 02:30 AM, we roused ourselves from slumber, prepared by 03:15 AM, and embarked on our journey around 03:30 AM, equipped with day packs and headlamps, our energy levels running high.

The Chandrashila Summit was no easy feat, but our determination propelled us onward. As we reached Tungnath temple, 1 km from the summit, breathless and resolute, we understood that climbing a mountain is a sensation you can only grasp by experiencing it first-hand. Reaching the summit at 3850 meters (12500 feet) was nothing short of extraordinary.

Chandrashila, as they say, is a gem nestled in the Himalayas. It showcases a kaleidoscope of landscapes throughout the seasons. In the spring, the region bursts into life as the trails leading to the summit are lined with vibrant rhododendron blooms and lush, green meadows. Summer unveils a lush and verdant panorama, with the meadows in full bloom and the trekking paths drenched in sunlight. Autumn bathes the landscape in warm golden hues as the leaves change, offering trekkers a striking contrast to the azure skies. When winter descends, Chandrashila transforms into a snow-clad wonderland, offering a serene and magical experience with its white landscape, blanketing the trees and trails in a pristine layer of snow. In every season, Chandrashila showcases its unique charm, promising a trekker's paradise and a nature lover's dream.

We lingered, absorbing the moment, and with half the mission accomplished, we descended to camp to recharge.

Day 4 – Chopta to Auli

After a hearty breakfast, we ventured towards Auli, a 5-6 hour drive away. Upon arrival, we checked into our guest house and received a briefing for the challenging 6-7 hour trek awaiting us the next day. Nestled in the lofty peaks of the Garhwal Himalayas, I must say, Auli is a winter wonderland.

Day 5 – Auli to Khulara

Following breakfast, we embarked on a taxing ascent, culminating in Khulara at 11220 feet after 6-8 hours of hiking. Our journey also led us to the summit of Kuari Pass, perched at 12870 feet, where we were bestowed with breathtaking views of the surrounding peaks. After savoring the vista, we returned to our camp.

Next in our journey loomed the formidable Pangarchulla Peak. Our Trek Leader advised an early morning start at 3:30 AM, given the strenuous climb that would scrutinize our endurance, determination, and physical fitness. An early dinner was on the menu to ensure we were well-rested for the impending challenge.

Day 6 – Khulara – Kuari Pass – Pangarchulla Summit

We rose at 2:30 AM, ready by 3:15 AM with day packs and headlamps illuminating our path. Our enthusiasm was palpable, but it wasn't long before the steep climb tested our resolve. At the 2 km mark, we paused, greeted by the sunrise and a 360-degree panorama featuring Dronagiri, Hathi Parbat, Ghoda Parvat, and a glimpse of the Pangarchulla peak.

The last 2 km were the most demanding, a relentless uphill battle. The final 250 meters were excruciating, but our determination fueled us, and at 8:00 AM, we triumphantly reached the summit at 4575 meters (15098 feet). The elation was indescribable. I unfurled the Indian Flag (Tiranga) and the BAoS banner, commemorating the moment in photographs. We relished the view, a profound testament to our achievement.

Day 6 – Khulara – Dhak – Joshimath

After a spell on the summit, we began our descent, winding through the dense forest to reach the village of Dhak. From there, a cab carried us to Joshimath, where we spent the night.

Day 7 – Joshimath – Rishikesh

Returning to Rishikesh after breakfast, we partook in the traditional Ganga Snan and evening Aarti, bidding a fond farewell to our remarkable journey. We reflected on the breathtaking trails, the bonds we had forged, and the indelible memories etched over the past days. The vistas of Deoria Tal, Chandrashila Summit, Chopta, Auli, the Kuari Pass, and the mighty Pangarchulla Summit will forever be cherished.

Mission accomplished. The story continues...

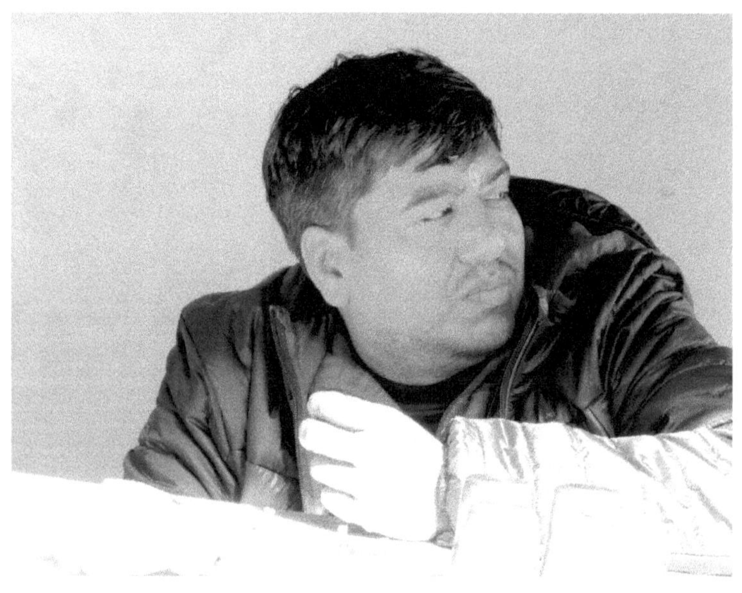

Three Musketeers' Himalayan Odyssey

Exploring new places is like unravelling hidden treasures in a world waiting to be discovered. For me, it's not just about travel; it's about embracing the unknown, diving into uncharted territories, and immersing myself in new experiences.

Back in early 2018, the idea of trekking sparked a flame within me. The thought of venturing into the heart of nature, surrounded by its raw beauty, thrilled me. I shared this dream with friends, envisioning an epic adventure in which 22 of us initially expressed interest. Yet, as time passed, discussions lingered, and plans remained elusive.

Driven by my eagerness to turn this dream into reality, I decided to take charge. I reached out to two friends and pitched the idea of the Kedarkantha trek in Uttarakhand. To my delight, they jumped at the opportunity, sharing my enthusiasm for this mountainous escapade. It was a decisive moment – the spark that reignited our dormant plans. Finally, after meticulous planning and unwavering determination, our dream transformed into a tangible plan.

The Kedarkantha trek, celebrated for its wintry charm and breathtaking panoramas, became our anticipated six-day endeavor, encompassing both the summit ascent and a side trip to Haridwar.

Two months of meticulous preparation preceded our journey, during which our daily routines transformed into a rigorous training regimen. We delved into a diverse fitness routine, embracing everything from brisk running sessions to tranquil walks and invigorating cycling jaunts. Each day, our focus was on fortifying ourselves physically and mentally, ensuring we'd be well-equipped to navigate the demanding terrain and relish the spectacular sights awaiting us in the Himalayas.

Our trio kicked off our adventure by creating a special group chat, where we shared workout plans, shopping tips, and bubbling excitement. Finally, the big day arrived, and we touched down in Delhi, feeling super pumped. Our first stop was the Akshardham temple, soaking in its peaceful vibes before heading to Connaught Place for a hearty dinner. After our meal, we wandered around the lively streets, soaking in the city buzz before making our way to catch our train from the railway station.

Bright and early in Dehradun the next morning, we met Kush, our trek leader, and the rest of the gang joining us on this expedition. It was awesome to see that everyone was friendly and ready for the trek! At that moment, with the sun rising over the town, it hit us: this trip was about more than just climbing mountains; it was about connecting with these amazing people and sharing this adventure together.

Day 1 was a long journey from Dehradun to Gaichan Gaon, taking about eight to nine hours by road, passing through scenic spots like Mussoorie. By late afternoon, around 4 o'clock, we finally rolled into Gaichan Gaon, a quaint village adorned with just a handful of houses. As the sun began its descent, all the trekkers had assembled in this tiny village. We huddled together in a cozy hall for our introduction session. It was like a mini melting pot - the Mumbai crew, the Oriya gang, the Singapore squad, the Kolkata group, and more.

Our trek leader, Kush, took charge and filled us in on the dos and don'ts, guiding us on how we'd be spending the upcoming days. He brought up this cool idea: 6-7-8, which meant tea at 6:00 AM, breakfast at 7:00 AM, and being ready to hit the trail by 8:00 AM. Kush also shared a new chant with us – "How's the Josh? High Kush!" It pumped up our spirits, making us super excited for the thrilling trek that lay ahead. This pep talk set the mood for what promised to be an incredible journey.

On Day 2, our journey took us from Gaichan Gaon at 5,600 feet to Jalouta at a lofty 8,950 feet, spanning a trek lasting around 4 to 6 hours. Fueled by a hearty breakfast at our starting point in Gaichan, we kicked off the day's adventure. Some of us lightened our load by entrusting our bags to mules, joining our trek leader Kush Bhai, local guides Mohan Bhai & Mukesh Bhai, and a cheerful troupe of dogs.

The trek was a mix of refreshing moments and energizing breaks. We refilled our water bottles at the basecamp, sipping on the crystal-clear, ice-cold water that refreshed our spirits as we ventured forward. Amidst the breathtaking scenery, we carried on, our backpacks holding our packed lunches. Passing through a village named Atwar, we paused to refuel with quick bites of Maggi and steaming tea, recharging our energy for the path ahead.

After about 5 to 6 hours of synchronized strides, covering 4 kilometers and ascending 3,350 feet in altitude, we finally arrived at the Jalouta camp. Nestled amidst a dense forest, our tents awaited, ready to provide shelter in this secluded haven. Here, the world beyond faded away; no screens, no calls, just nature's embrace.

Gathering together, we unwound with a brief exercise session, renewing our spirits with each "How's the JOSH - HIGH KUSH?" chant, keeping our enthusiasm soaring for the adventures yet to unfold.

On Day 3, we began our trek from Jalouta in the early morning, navigating a steep path toward Pukhrola, standing tall at 10,800 feet. The climb was a test of endurance, taking us about 4 to 5 hours to cover the 1,850 feet in altitude gain. Despite the summit appearing deceptively close from Pukhrola, the actual distance was quite different.

Amidst this challenging trek, a unique moment unfolded. I found myself engaged in an impromptu cricket match, a thrilling experience at such a high altitude. As evening descended, the night sky at Pukhrola camp was simply indescribable, its beauty transcending any words I could muster. Under this enchanting sky, Kush Bhai briefed us about the plans for the following day, prompting us to set our alarms for a very early start at 2:30 AM.

On Day 4, our journey began long before the first light kissed the sky. At 2:30 AM, we stirred from our slumber, gearing up by 3:15 AM. Equipped with our day packs and headlamps, we set out at 3:30 AM, fueled by a reservoir of determination. The path to the Kedarkantha Summit wasn't a walk in the park. Each step felt like an eternity, the peak tauntingly close yet seemingly unreachable. But we persisted, echoing the mantra "HIGH KUSH," propelling ourselves forward until, finally, we stood atop the summit at 12,500 feet (3850 meters). Words fell short in capturing that triumphant moment of reaching the pinnacle.

The elation of achievement enveloped us as we savored the breathtaking views, capturing timeless snapshots with our team and the fluttering Indian flag. After relishing our triumph, we commenced our descent. Amidst the journey back, the snowy slopes beckoned us to indulge in some playful slides, guided by the expertise of Kush Bhai, Mohan Bhai, and Mukesh Bhai, a unique and thrilling experience indeed.

Post a satisfying lunch, we descended from Pukhrola to Akroti

Thach camp. Our trek leaders, Kush Bhai, along with guides Mohan Bhai & Mukesh Bhai, showcased unwavering dedication, ensuring each step of our adventure was unforgettable. Their tireless efforts enriched our trek, and we owe them gratitude for their exceptional guidance and support throughout this remarkable journey.

On Day 5, our footsteps retraced the path back to base camp, signaling the near end of our expedition. What had commenced as a trek among three friends from Singapore had blossomed into a family of over 30 individuals by April 12th. The camaraderie that evolved along the trails was a testament to the bond forged during our adventurous escapade.

On Day 6, our journey back to Dehradun marked the final leg of our expedition. The winding roads led us through Gaichan, Mussoorie, and Haridwar before reaching our destination. Before bidding adieu to this enriching journey, we made a poignant stop at Haridwar. The Ganga Snan, a sacred dip in the holy waters of the Ganges, and the captivating evening Aarati left an indelible mark on our hearts. Savoring the renowned Lassi of Haridwar added a delightful touch to our memorable day before we set off for Dehradun.

As the curtain fell on our expedition, we bid farewell to the picturesque trails, the arduous paths we conquered, the friendships that blossomed, and the remarkable landscapes that etched themselves in our memories. The legacy of our journey continued, an unwritten story woven through the majestic woods, mountains, and the enchanting Kedarkantha Peak, a tale waiting to be told in every step forward.

Aurko KK, '18

CHAPTER FOUR

Conquering Mount Ophir's Heights

"Mountains teach that not all paths are meant to be walked; some are meant to be climbed."

Life is like a big adventure, right? I think it's super important to keep that adventurous spirit alive—it's what keeps us happy! My adventure journey kicked off back in August 2018. Me and my pals were chatting about going on a trek somewhere outside of Singapore. We tossed ideas around for about two weeks without deciding on anything concrete. But I didn't lose hope. Finally, we settled on a day trek to Mount Ophir.

This mountain, also known as Gunung Ledang, stands tall at 1276 meters and sits up in northwest Johor, Malaysia. It's quite a popular and tough climb over there!

Remember that quote from John Muir?

The mountains are calling, and I must go!

So, after some back-and-forth, a solid gang of 15 of us signed up for this one-day trek up Mount Ophir. It was all about gearing up for this brand-new adventure. But hey, trekking? It's no walk in the park. We had to be in tip-top shape! So, we dove into a month-long hustle of running, walking, doing squats, and all sorts of workout routines. We had to get ourselves ready for that climb!

To really nail this prep, we got serious about sharing stuff. We swapped exercise routines, made shopping lists, and kept the hype up with our excitement levels off the charts. Some folks even shared stories from their previous treks and dropped motivational quotes to keep us all amped. Remember that Helen Keller line? "Alone, we can do so little; together, we can do so much." That was the vibe!

And then, finally, the big day arrived! The one we'd been waiting for!

We had this super detailed plan mapped out for the day, and boy, did we stick to it like glue! Alarm clocks blaring at 2:30 AM, we sprang into action, got ourselves ready, and hit the meeting spot dead-on by 4:00 AM. That's how we roll! By around 4:30 AM, we were off and running, landing at the base camp by 7:30 AM sharp.

The local guide was all about laying down the law—rules, regulations, and the game plan for our trek. We kicked off the actual climb around 8:30 AM, armed with our daypacks, headlamps, and enough snacks to power a rocket ship. And let me tell you, that summit? It wasn't messing around. The path felt never-ending, and every time we asked the guide how much farther, it was always the same old' "just two more hours" spiel. Talk about a trek that felt like forever!

But you know what? Even when the peak seemed right there, yet so far away, we stuck to our guns with this "WILL DO" attitude. We just kept pushing ahead, cheering each other on, and refusing to give in. It was all about that mutual support, keeping the fire alive in each other's bellies!

We kicked off that morning with all the pep and excitement in the world, but man, let me tell you, when we hit that 1 km mark before the summit, we were running on empty. Mount Ophir might not be the tallest peak around these parts, but don't let that fool you—it's a tough nut to crack. Ladders, ropes, scrambling—this mountain threw it all at us.

By the time 2:30 PM rolled around, we finally made it to the tippy-top. And wow, that feeling? It's like nothing I can put into words. The sense of accomplishment was off the charts! This whole experience, it was something else entirely, you know? And we owe every bit of it to the incredible teamwork and that never-say-die attitude we brought along. Earl Nightingale had it spot on when he said, "All you need is the plan, the road map, and the courage to press on to your destination." And boy, did we have that roadmap and courage in spades. It's what got us to that finish line!

After soaking in the breathtaking views and revelling in our triumph at the top, we gathered around for a homemade feast. Greg Child hit the nail on the head when he said, "Somewhere between the bottom and the summit is the answer to the mystery of why we climb." And let me tell you, that lunch felt like a victory banquet fit for champions! Then, around 3:30 PM, it was time for those iconic group photos—a way to seal this epic moment in time.

Throughout the entire trek, every single one of us, all 15 team members, had each other's backs. It was this unshakeable support and constant cheerleading that propelled us safely to that summit. We cheered for every little victory, big or small. But hey, let's not forget, this journey was a serious test of grit. Nearly 24 hours without sleep, pushing our bodies and minds to the max—this trek pushed us harder than anything else we've faced.

But you know what? Despite the exhaustion and the uphill battles (literally!), it was a ride we wouldn't trade for the world. After a solid breather at base camp, we bid adieu to this adventure and headed back to our regular routines. This climb? One for the record books.

Saying goodbye is always the toughest part. It's time to bid adieu to the breathtaking paths we trekked, the trails we conquered, the moments we held dear, the memories we made, and the whole shebang—the woods, the forests, the mountains, and that majestic peak of Mount Ophir.

During our trek, some words of wisdom really stuck with us. Kiran had this gem: "It's all a mental game; if it was physical, we could have collapsed." And Sachin dropped this one: "When pain crosses the threshold, it hurts no more." Those words kept us going when the going got tough.

One of our gang, Rajesh, summed up this journey in such a beautiful way:

Unexplainable body pain
The soul feels fresh and energetic
My heart feels light with pride of achievement
A permanent grin on the face that doesn't want to fade away
My bed feels like heaven

Closed eyes don't wish to go back to reality
Get a chance will go again to the Summit
With a group of high-energy friends
Multi-dimensional expertise and gurus
Where else can we learn my practical MBA?

Minimalist theories from Shiv
Yoga lessons from Mamta Deshmukh
Inner engineering knowledge from Kiran
Situational leadership from Pritesh
Everybody is an expert in different ways. Where else can we learn

all in one place?

One goal to reach the Summit
There was no apparent leadership training
With the various fitness levels and perspectives
We conquered Mt. Ophir! Hurray!
Let's push our limit to new heights soon!

Mountain Echoes: Trials and Triumphs on Mount Belumut

Setting off on a trek is like diving into an unforgettable adventure, one that leaves an indelible mark on your soul. It's not just about the destination; it's the whole thrilling journey that begs to be cherished. Stepping out of our comfort zones is where the real lessons about ourselves unfold—it takes courage, but it's worth it.

The Bhagavad Gita's wisdom, when applied to the context of marathons and trekkings, offers a powerful perspective on life: It is not the destination that defines us but the way we travel the path. It encourages us to embrace each step with faith, to persevere through difficulties with detachment from the outcome, and to find inner strength and peace in the knowledge that every journey is a step towards self-discovery and spiritual growth.

Both marathons and trekkings encapsulate the Gita's teachings on karma yoga—the path of selfless action. They teach us to engage fully in our pursuits, to face challenges with courage, and to find joy in the effort itself. These activities remind us that while goals are important, true fulfillment comes from the journey, the lessons learned, and the growth experienced along the way.

As Susan Jagannath so aptly put it, "The mountain has been calling me, and it's time to answer."

Our escapade kicked off in early January 2019, a quest to seize our first trek of the year despite time constraints. Having triumphed over Mount Ophir the previous year, we craved more challenges and fresh adventures near Johor. Our search led us to uncover a one-day trek to Mount Belumut. The excitement was palpable.

Mount Belumut, also known as Gunung Belumut, proudly stands at 1,010 meters, a striking presence near Kluang town in Malaysia's Johor state. But let me tell you, this climb? It's no walk in the park.

Planning for this trek felt like hitting the reset button for me. We initially had a solid crew of 15 all set for this one-day adventure up Mount Belumut. To ensure we all had a blast and a successful climb, we kicked things into gear to prep ourselves. But you know what's awesome? The enthusiasm of the initial crew was so infectious that 19 more folks jumped in to join the trek! Talk about a growing team spirit!

We understood that trekking demands serious physical effort, so we didn't take it lightly. For a good two months leading up to the big day, we put our muscles through the wringer—lots of running, walking, and all sorts of exercises. 'Cause let's face it, when it comes to trekking, having a fit body and an active mind is the golden ticket to reaching that finish line.

Confucius rightly said, "A man who does not plan long ahead will find trouble at his door."

As we prepped for the trek, we were all about that sharing vibe. We tossed around exercise routines, made joint shopping lists, and amped up each other's excitement levels. Motivational quotes and tales from past treks? Oh yeah, those were flying around too. And talk about teamwork—some of us lent gear to those in need, making sure everyone was fully equipped for the adventure.

But you know how it goes. About a week before the big day, a bunch of pals who'd done this trek before started sharing their stories and flashing their photos. It got a few of the newer folks feeling a bit down in the dumps. Thankfully, we quickly hit the mental reset button. We rallied together, chanting our unofficial mantra: "HOW is JOSH?" It was like a magic spell, instantly recharging everyone's batteries and boosting our confidence sky-high for the trek. That phrase became our battle cry through it all.

All set and raring to go, we converged at three different pickup spots, all revved up for our big adventure.

We had this meticulous plan laid out to ensure everything ran like clockwork. Rise and shine at 3:00 AM, gear up, and assemble at the meet-up point by 4:15 AM. But, uh-oh, the transport for the first bunch hit a snag—it got delayed by a whole hour, thanks to picking up people from different spots. Talk about a domino effect! Panic started rippling through the gang because, you know, time was ticking and schedules were getting all topsy-turvy.

Quick thinking became our superpower at that moment. We had to keep the show on the road! So, in a snap decision, we rerouted the first group of trekkers to kick off their adventure pronto, guided by just one of our experts. It was a lesson in handling the unexpected, teaching us the importance of keeping the momentum going, no matter what curveballs life throws. And you know what? Our teamwork and positive vibes? They swooped in like superheroes, saving the day by solving the problem on the fly.

The hiccups just kept on coming. The second bunch of trekkers? They got hit with a two-hour transport delay too. You could practically taste the panic in the air. Some folks even started asking for refunds and tossing out negative reviews. But hey, despite the storm clouds, we held onto our positivity and focused on what lay ahead—the adventure waiting for us.

But wait, there's more! The saga continued. At the emigration point, more delays reared their pesky heads, and to top it off, our driver took a detour into Lostville. That mishap tacked on a whopping four extra hours to our journey, throwing our plans of reaching the summit together and snapping that epic group photo right out the window. Cue the collective sighs of frustration and disappointment.

Yet, onwards we trudged, inching closer to that summit. The terrain? It turned into this serious challenge, pushing our bodies and minds to their limits. But you know what kept us going? Nature shows off its finest views at every turn. The sheer beauty of it all was our fuel, transporting us away from the ordinary grind. Sure, we were beaten, but that feeling of being amidst nature's grandeur? Priceless.

As we neared that elusive peak, exhaustion clung to us like a second skin. But guess what? We made it! That moment of reaching the top? Words fail to capture it. We soaked in the view, snapped photos galore, and busted out the snacks and drinks we'd stashed in our trusty daypacks. It was a slice of heaven, that moment of pure contentment. We stood proud, toasting ourselves for conquering this trek against all odds.

At the outset, we were bubbling with energy and excitement. But by the time we hit CP2—just halfway through the entire trek—our gusto had dwindled to near-empty. We regrouped, aiming to shuffle smaller clusters of trekkers onwards, determined to rally everyone toward reaching that summit and ensuring everyone's safe return.

Now, covering the ground from CP2 to CP3 took us a good hour, but honestly, we were still running on fumes. It was time for a breather, a lunch break where we bared our struggles, discussing the tough choices looming ahead. Some of us faced that daunting fork in the road—continue the upward slog or retreat to base camp due to the ticking clock. Two decided to call it a day, opting for the downward journey, while the majority soldiered on, pressing ahead to CP4.

For some, that pit stop offered a chance to recharge those batteries, reigniting the determination to push forward. By 4 PM, a fraction of us had made it 25% up CP4, only to have our guide intervene, redirecting us back to base camp. It was a sobering moment, a reminder that the clock had run its course, urging us to return to our regular lives.

And so, with heads held high but hearts heavy with the unfinished climb, we descended, knowing it was time to bid adieu to this adventure and return to the rhythm of our everyday routines.

Mount Belumut might not be the tallest peak in Southeast Asia, but let me tell you, it's a tough nut to crack. The natural landscape throws some seriously steep slopes—picture 80-degree climbs that'll give your legs a workout like no other.

Most of our gang managed to conquer that summit, though in smaller clusters. And let me just say the whole experience? Pure awesomeness! Huge props to the team for sticking together, and showcasing that never-give-up spirit that got us through those challenging slopes. Once at the top, they kicked back, taking in the breathtaking views and revelling in their hard-earned victory. Lunch at the summit was a collective effort, with everyone bringing up their share of goodies from home. And you know the rule—a summit without a group photo? Incomplete! So, they took a moment to capture that triumphant moment.

As the day wound down, all of us made it back safely to base camp, a journey filled with mutual support and encouragement every step of the way. Despite the hurdles thrown our way, we nailed it! We marked the achievement with cheers, pats on the back, and a well-deserved rest back at base camp. Victory never felt sweeter.

This day pushed us to our limits—no sleep for almost a full day, testing both our bodies and minds in ways we'd never imagined.

And now, it's that bittersweet moment again, bidding adieu to the incredible paths we trod, the trails we conquered in mere hours, the friendships forged in a single day, the shared memories, and the whole enchilada—the forests, the mountains, and that tough Mount Belumut trek.

After a hearty dinner in Kluang, we hit the road homeward. During the journey, we shared stories from our epic trek.

For some, this trek was a masterclass in the mind-body tango—Pritesh Shah summed it up perfectly. Priyanka Jaiswal's tale painted a picture of a journey that had its highs and lows. Kunal Dubey credited mental strength and teamwork for summiting. And Manoj Pandey found inspiration and personal growth in the trek.

The mission? Accomplished. But the story? Well, that's far from over...

Peak Pursuits: Tales of 5 Trek

You know that saying "Do what you love"? Well, for me, that's all about trekking. There's something magical about it that pulls me in every time. I just can't get enough of it! I'm always up for organizing treks and leading the pack. It's like my ultimate adventure.

So, I was on the lookout for a new trekking spot, and guess what? I stumbled upon this amazing 5 Peak Challenge in Malaysia. The idea of conquering Bukit Payung, Bukit Bandkuit, Bukit Alam, Bukit Botak, and Bukit Berdir in just one day got me all excited.

Now, these peaks might not tower over the clouds, standing at only 258 meters above sea level, but hey, don't let their height fool you. They might be small in size, but they pack a punch! The trek was a rollercoaster, starting with this steep climb that tested my legs and ending with an equally challenging slope down.

Barry Finlay once said, "Every mountain top is within reach if you just keep climbing." And you know what? That sums up my trekking journey perfectly. It's not just about reaching the peak; it's about the thrill of the climb, the breathtaking views, and the joy of pushing your limits.

Trekking? It's not just a hobby for me; it's a passion that keeps me reaching for those peaks, one step at a time.

Getting a team together for our next trek was our big task. I took charge and got busy rounding up at least 10 folks who were eager to join in. Organizing everything became my job—I was on it, sorting out all the details for the trek. It took a good two weeks to get everyone on board and finish up all the needed stuff.

Being the one who loves to plan and lead, I was over the moon when we got a team of 11 pumped-up trekkers ready for our day-long adventure. But hey, trekking needs some serious physical effort, so we didn't waste any time. We prepped for three whole weeks ahead of the trek. Running, walking, climbing stairs— you name it, we did it, just to make sure we were all set for the challenge that lay ahead.

On May 11th, 2019, our gang of 11 eager trekkers hopped onto the bus, all pumped up for the adventure ahead. Lucky for us, the journey went super smooth—no delays, just excitement brewing.

We kicked off our trek from the base camp, carrying our daypacks, and in about an hour, we hit our first mountain. The view was breathtaking! We paused for a bit, soaking in the beauty, snapping some photos before marching on to the next peak. But with each climb, our energy took a nosedive.

The second mountain welcomed us with open arms, and boy, were we ready for a break! Lunchtime was a relief—we shared stories, unloaded our backpacks, and laughed our tiredness away. Jokes flew around, lifting our spirits and refueling us for the rest of the trek. Together, we conquered those remaining mountains, and then it was time to make our way back down to base camp. That marked the end of our trek—a bittersweet reminder that our normal lives awaited us.

This trek was something else! What made it special was how we stuck together, all 11 of us, through thick and thin, from start to finish. And you know what? We nailed it—we conquered all 5 mountains, achieved our goal, and got back home safe and sound. What an awesome experience! Big shoutout to the team for their amazing teamwork and never-give-up attitude. Everyone was super enthusiastic, supportive, and kept each other going strong until we safely made it back to base camp.

To sum up this epic journey, I'd go with Harley King's words: "May your dreams be larger than mountains and may you have the courage to scale their summits." That quote speaks volumes to me as a trekker. Our goals should be as grand as those towering mountains, and we should always dare to reach their peaks. We celebrated our triumph at base camp, soaking in the moderate trek and relishing the stunning nature around us.

As the day wound down, it was time to say goodbye to the amazing paths we trekked, the bonds we forged, the stories we shared, and the breathtaking forests and mountains we explored. We grabbed dinner in @JB and then headed back home, cherishing every moment of this unforgettable adventure.

Finishing a mission always feels great!

Here's a quote I love:

Trekking is an adventure that, once you are into it, you cannot get out of you. It is also fun that you need to enjoy. You need the courage to step out of your comfort zone, and that's when you learn more about yourselves.

CHAPTER SEVEN

A Day To Remember

The seashores are gorgeous, aren't they? Who wouldn't love a chance to stroll along those stunning coastlines? Singapore's Coast to Coast (C2C) walk is a brilliant way to promote a healthy lifestyle. We all know that good health is like a treasure—it's the key to a great life. Ever since its launch on March 30, 2019, completing this 36 KM trail in Singapore has been a dream for enthusiastic walkers. Count me in—I'm always eager to step up for the global step challenge, and the C2C trail seemed like the perfect fit.

Dennis Wilson's words ring so true: "On the beach, you can live in bliss." There's something truly magical about the beach!

Walking 36 kilometers isn't everyone's thing, but I was blown away by the 10+ enthusiastic trekkers—friends and family—who were all in for this adventure. It was heart-warming to see their interest in experiencing this unique journey with me. As we geared up for the walk, we made sure to go over the guidelines before hitting the trail. First up on the to-do list was grabbing the 'NParks Coast-to-Coast mobile app. This little buddy was our guide, helping us navigate through the different checkpoints along the trail.

As we trekked along, a few of our companions chose to head back, but the rest of us kept on, enjoying each other's company, the stunning nature surrounding us, and a string of light-hearted jokes. We crossed CP3 at Hindhede Drive, which meant about 3000 steps, and then CP4 at Botanic Gardens, a whopping 7000 steps—almost halfway through the trail. Some of our crew decided it was time to call it a day there. But not us! The six of us left were dead set on completing this trek. Around 8:45 PM, we grabbed a quick bite to eat, even though our bodies were pretty worn out, and pushed on toward CP5 at Bishan-Ang Mo Kio Park. It was a tough stretch—nearly 3 hours and roughly 10,000 steps—but we finally made it to CP5 by 11:30 PM. There, two more of our group decided it was the end of the road for them.

The determination of the final four of us was put to the test. We faced a crucial decision—should we push on or call it quits? We chose to keep going, and once we made that call, there was no looking back. CP6, CP7, and finally CP8 were our checkpoints, totaling around 16,000 steps. It was a grueling 11-hour journey to cover the entire 38.2 kilometers, and we wrapped it up around 2:00 AM on June 23. I'll be honest, those last 200 meters were tough. Each step felt like a monumental feat. At CP8, we took a well-deserved breather, lying on the ground for a good 30 minutes before heading back home. That night's adventure left a mark on all of us. The next morning dawned, and you could feel a different kind of energy in the air, each of us filled with memories of the epic trek. Big cheers to everyone who participated, but a special shoutout to the last four troopers—Shiv, Manish, Vivek, and Amit—for their incredible dedication. Can't wait for the next C2C walk, hoping for an even bigger turnout.

Some of us shared our experiences.

To walk far, walk together – Manish.
Tiredness and Craziness have no relation – Amit Giri
Mental strength is a key to success. – Shiv
Indeed, it was the Mind which kept us going – Vivek

Singapore Botanic Gardens
Bukit Timah Gate

Trek to Kota Tinggi

On a quiet July 3rd, 2019, as I sipped my morning coffee and pondered over my affection for trekking, a quote by J.R.R. Tolkien caught my eye: "Not all those who wander are lost." It struck a chord, reminding me that it had been nearly two months since our last trek. My mind drifted through the memories of past adventures, stirring up the itch for another escapade.

Considering I'd taken the lead for our last three treks, I felt it was time to hand over the reins to someone else in our group. That's when Sanjay, a seasoned trekker among us, stepped up to lead this expedition.

We embarked on a joint quest to scout out new territories, seeking fresh landscapes to explore. After a solid week of scouring options, Sanjay pitched the idea of a day trek to Kota Tinggi—a suggestion that sparked our collective interest.

Mount Panti stands tall at 531 meters, just a short distance north of Kota Tinggi, a town located in the state of Johor, Malaysia, which derives its name from its historical and geographical significance. The name "Kota Tinggi" can be translated to "High Fort" or "High City" in English, reflecting its historical role as a defensive and administrative centre.

The fortification and the town that grew around it played a

significant role in the early history of the Johor Sultanate, serving as a capital and a stronghold during its formative years. Over time, the name Kota Tinggi came to signify not just the physical fortifications but also the area's stature as an important centre in the historical narrative of Johor.

Today, while the fortifications no longer exist, the name Kota Tinggi remains, reflecting the town's rich historical heritage and its importance in the historical development of the Johor Sultanate and Malaysia as a whole. What makes it even more enticing is the stunning waterfall nestled close to the base camp.

Sanjay's plan to trek to Mount Panti and relish the waterfall got everyone buzzing with excitement. I've always had a soft spot for waterfalls. They have this incredible way of showcasing Mother Nature's beauty. As We Dream of Travel wisely pointed out, "Amazing how a thundering water can be so violent and calming at once."

Our next challenge: rounding up a team of 10 to 15 eager adventurers. Sanjay took charge, rallying and inspiring folks to join in, and boy, did he do a stellar job! He managed to bring together an incredible crew, including skilled individuals like photographers Rakesh Chauhan and Saurabh Srivastav, who also doubled as a video editor. We even had TikTok influencers Mamta Sharma & Harsh Ranjan and a singer, Saurabh Srivastav, adding their unique talents to the mix.

What made our gang so awesome was our diversity. We hailed from different corners, each bringing our flair to the team, making it a beautiful blend of skills and backgrounds.

Knowing that trekking demanded some serious physical effort, we prepped ourselves. For weeks, we made running, walking, and those up-and-down vertical exercises a part of our daily routines. Gotta make sure those muscles were ready for the adventure!

On August 17, 2019, our group of 12 eager trekkers gathered from different spots, all set to embark on a shared adventure. Lucky for us, our journey went off without a hitch—no delays, just smooth sailing. After a 2-3 hour ride, we finally arrived at the base camp, where our guide welcomed us and dished out a quick rundown of the mountain and a safety briefing.

With spirits high, we set off toward our ultimate goal—the summit. Scaling a mountain means getting those legs moving, and let me tell you, it was a good four-hour trek to reach that peak. The hike itself was moderate, a pleasant stroll that we managed pretty comfortably. But here's the twist: those slippery boulders were a challenge! We found ourselves crawling and scrambling along logs, and at one point, we even had to make use of a rope. It was like a four-hour journey through the untamed Kota Tinggi rainforest.

Finally, we conquered that summit! High-fives all around, a bunch of photos clicked, and then it was time to settle down for a well-deserved lunch. And boy, was it a feast! We had dishes from different cuisines, a real treat for our taste buds. As we dug in, we pondered over that famous quote, "The best view comes after the hardest climb." And let me tell you, that view from the summit? Breathtaking! It left us all in awe, lost for words in the beauty of it all.

As we began our descent back to base camp, the anticipation for the nearby waterfall grew. And let me tell you, it was everything we hoped for and more. Refreshing waters, pure fun, and the most rejuvenating experience awaited us. The sound of the water crashing down was like a gentle symphony, drowning out the noise of the world around us. For that moment, we were entirely lost in the embrace of nature's beauty.

This trek? It was something else. And the best part? The incredible group I shared it with. We were a tight-knit bunch, always there for each other. Our team spirit, that never-give-up attitude? That's what carried us through every challenge this trek threw our way. Saying farewell to the paths we walked, the trails we left our mark on, and the memories we etched together filled us with a sense of pride, satisfaction, and pure happiness.

Before bidding adieu, we made a pit stop at JB to taste their famed parathas, and let me tell you, they were beyond amazing—some of the best we'd ever had! With our bellies full and hearts brimming with joy, we headed back home, thankful for the unforgettable adventure we shared.

As Sir Edmund Hillary rightly put it, "It is not the mountain we conquer but ourselves." And on this trek, we conquered so much more than just the trail.

CHAPTER NINE

Stair Climbing Challenge

For me, trying out new things is like adding a dash of positivity to life's recipe. It was smack in the middle of December 2019 when I felt that itch for a fresh adventure in the world of sports. And you know what popped into my head? Stair-climbing! Now, I wasn't in it for a test of my physical prowess or to join any race. Been there, done that—tackled stair climbing and even aced the Swiss vertical marathons in Singapore three times in a row.

This time around, my aim wasn't about proving anything to anyone. Nah. It was all about challenging myself, venturing into new territories, and soaking up experiences I hadn't dived into before.

As Bhavya Choudhary wisely said, "Try new things and discover yourself every single day." That struck a chord with me. I wanted to embark on a stair-climbing journey lasting three months—an adventure I could share with everyone. My goal? To conquer at least 20+ floors (that's about 500+ stairs) every week. But that wasn't all. I committed to hitting a minimum of 10,000 steps daily and keeping up with regular cycling.

In my book, faith plays a crucial role in reaching our goals. Martin Luther King Jr. captured it perfectly: "Faith is taking the first step even when you don't see the whole staircase." It's that leap of faith, that trust in ourselves and the journey ahead, even when it's not crystal clear.

So, on December 27, 2019, I embarked on my first climb—a challenge of 21 floors. Here's what I learned in that initial week: Starting is key. Getting that ball rolling, and finding a reason to take that first step—it's what sets the journey in motion. And once you've begun, it's all about progress. It's a continuous journey, always moving forward once you've made that start.

In the seventh week of my stair-climbing saga, a colleague decided to jump aboard the routine train. Suddenly, it was the dynamic duo tackling the stairs together. This brought me to my next lesson: the importance of keeping that momentum going. Progress became our companion on this journey. Sure, there were moments when I felt like calling it quits on this weekly ritual. But you know what kept me going? The drive to finish what I started, to complete this story I was crafting. Your "why" should be strong enough to shield you from thoughts of throwing in the towel.

When I conquered the 10th week, reaching the peak and capturing a selfie up there, a rush of pride and achievement washed over me. Reflecting on this whole experience, a light bulb went off in my head. You know what's toughest? Starting! Summoning the motivation and finding that crystal-clear reason why you're doing something—that's the real challenge at the beginning. Progressing is no piece of cake either. Many folks throw in the towel when they hit that wall. But here's the kicker: completing even a small part of the journey sparks a sense of triumph and joy. It's not about the size of the accomplishment; it's about how it makes you feel. Happiness blooms from completing the journey and crafting a tale worth sharing.

The stair-climbing journey taught me a vital lesson: "Stair Climbing helps to boost the stamina and allows you to unlock your hidden energy." It's proof that every journey starts with that one crucial step forward.

Every journey begins with just a single step.

Conquering Singapore's Round Island Route: A Month-Long Adventure

Singapore's Round Island Route (RIR) is like a green belt wrapping around the city, a 150-kilometer trail that's part urban explorer, part nature enthusiast's dream. Imagine having the ultimate pass to discover hidden gems, from bustling cityscapes to tranquil green hideaways and coastal breezes, all in one seamless loop. It's the island's way of showing off how effortlessly it can blend skyscrapers with greenery, making every step (or pedal) an adventure in its own right.

This grand loop is more than just a path; it's Singapore's bold statement on living in harmony with nature, transforming the "City in a Garden" vision into a walkable, cyclable reality. Whether you're in it for the fitness, the scenery, or a bit of cultural discovery, the RIR is your go-to for experiencing the diverse vibes of Singapore. It's the city's open invitation to explore, connect, and see for yourself how it balances the buzz of development with the serenity of nature, all in a day's walk.

Our plan? Conquer this 150 km RIR within just a month—from October 1st to October 31st, 2020. Now, that's a challenge!

To make this happen, we had to do a couple of things. First up, we needed to track the entire route using GPS. And oh, here's the fun part—we had to snap selfies at 15 different checkpoints along the way. Wanna know where these checkpoints were? Hang on, here's the list:

- Woodlands Jetty
- Sembawang Hotspring
- Coney Island (West Entrance)
- Lorong Halus Jetty
- Changi Village Hawker Center
- Sunrise View
- Bedok Jetty
- Bay East Garden Visitor Center
- ArtScience Museum
- Resort World Sentosa
- Southernmost Point of Continental Asia
- Henderson Waves
- McDonald's West Coast Park
- Johor Strait Lighthouse
- Sungei Buloh Wetland Reserve

Phew! That's quite a checklist, right? But hey, these spots were like little milestones along the way, marking our progress as we circled the island.

Manoj Pandey joined me on this month-long trek, and we had a smart plan. Instead of tackling the whole route in one go, we decided to break it down into nine days, taking on smaller chunks of the journey each day.

Our adventure began on October 4th, kicking off from Changi Village Hawker Center and making our way to Bedok Jetty—a stretch of about 24 kilometers. That day, we crossed off two checkpoints: Sunrise View and Bedok Jetty. And you know what we did at each checkpoint? Yep, you guessed it—we captured a selfie to mark our conquest! After a bit of a breather and some well-deserved rest, we headed back home, ready to tackle the next leg of our trek.

Then came October 7th, and we covered a shorter distance, trekking from Coney Island's West Entrance to Downtown East Pasir Ris, covering around 14 kilometers. This leg brought us past two more checkpoints: Lorong Halus Jetty and Coney Island's West Entrance. We made sure to snap those checkpoint selfies, capturing the milestones we hit along the way, before heading back home for some relaxation.

On October 10th, I embarked on a solo trek from Downtown East Pasir Ris to Changi Village Hawker Center, covering about 6 kilometers. It was a breezy stroll, and along the way, I conquered another checkpoint: Changi Village Hawker Center. One step closer, one checkpoint down!

The following day, October 11th, we took on a longer stretch, trekking from Bedok Jetty to Vivocity, clocking in roughly 19 kilometers. This leg was quite a haul, marking off two more checkpoints: Bay East Garden Visitor Center and ArtScience Museum. Phew, that was a tough one! We were pretty pooped by the end, feeling the fatigue kick in, making it even a bit challenging to snap a photo.

By this point, we had triumphed over seven checkpoints, which gave us a real boost of confidence. It felt like we were hitting our stride and were confident we could conquer the entire walk within the given time frame.

Then came October 15th, and we covered a moderate distance from

McDonald's West Coast Park to VivoCity, totaling around 16 kilometers. This part of the trek checked off four more checkpoints: Resort World Sentosa, McDonald's West Coast Park, the Southernmost Point of Continental Asia, and Henderson Waves. We made sure to grab a selfie at each checkpoint to celebrate our progress. And you know what? Along the way, I even had a quick tea break, catching up with friends while continuing our journey. A little relaxation and some friendly chatter made the walk even more enjoyable.

On October 18th, we embarked on a brisk walk from Kranji MRT to Coney Island's West Entrance, a journey spanning about 25 kilometers. This leg unlocked two more checkpoints: Woodlands Jetty and Sembawang Hotspring. With each checkpoint, we made sure to pause, snap a selfie, and soak up the joy of our progress. The walk itself? Oh, it was delightful!

Moving on to October 21st, we opted for a moderate walk from Kranji MRT to Boon Lay MRT, passing through the stunning Sungei Buloh Wetland Reserve, covering roughly 23 kilometers. This leg completed one more checkpoint: Sungei Buloh Wetland. Again, we captured those milestone selfies and relished every step of our journey.

At this point, we were inching closer to our goal, having almost conquered 14 checkpoints, which amounted to roughly 125 kilometers covered within just 21 days. Talk about determination and progress!

Fast forward to October 26th, when we undertook a moderate stroll from Boon Lay MRT to Tuas Link MRT via Johor Straight Lighthouse, a distance of approximately 15 kilometers. Hitting the Johor Straight Lighthouse checkpoint felt like another triumph, and naturally, we made sure to capture the moment with another selfie. Each step brought us closer to our finish line, and we were loving every minute of it.

And then came the ultimate day, October 30th! We embarked on a final moderate walk from Tuas Link MRT to McDonald's West Coast, covering about 22 kilometers. This leg marked the triumphant completion of our 150 km Round Island Route trek. Can you believe it? Our planning was spot on, and our execution was impeccable. Not only did we conquer the intended distance, but we even went beyond, clocking in over 160 kilometers throughout this incredible trek. And you know what? Every step was filled with laughter, camaraderie, and a whole lot of fun.

Takeaway:

"Perfect planning and execution are crucial to achieving your goal. Your passion will drive you towards your goal."
-Shiv

CHAPTER ELEVEN

Strides Together: Building Fitness and Community with Fun4walk

In the digital age, staying fit has gotten a tech-savvy makeover, making excuses harder to come by and fitness more fun than a barrel of emoji. Health apps have turned our smartphones into mini fitness gurus, nagging us to move more, eat better, and sleep longer—kind of like a pocket-sized mom, minus the "I told you so." From counting steps to brewing up personalized workout potions, these apps keep us on our toes, quite literally, and ensure our health game is as strong as our meme game.

Then there's WhatsApp, the unsung hero of group fitness. It's where we rally the troops for morning jogs, swap kale smoothie recipes (that we swear we'll try "tomorrow"), and share our victories, no matter how small. These groups are less about showing off and more about showing up—for ourselves and each other. It turns out, a little peer pressure can be a good thing, especially if it's nudging us towards that extra push-up or a healthier lunch.

The idea for Fun4walk sprouted from my own resolutions for 2023. I was keen on not only enhancing our fitness but also giving back to our community. Health, especially as we grow older, becomes pivotal in our lives, and taking care of it is non-negotiable. Luckily, this initiative struck a chord with 20 enthusiastic individuals who were eager to join in.

To make Fun4walk effective, we chose the Pacer tool to track our steps and created a WhatsApp group for seamless data sharing and mutual motivation. We framed a 30-day step challenge for the community with simple yet achievable rules:

Everyone aimed for a minimum of 5,000 steps daily.

The challenge capped at a maximum of 15,000 steps per day.

However, as with any new venture, we encountered a minor hiccup on day one. One participant left the group feeling a bit disheartened after being nudged away from casual chatting. It's a reminder that in steering a group toward common goals, maintaining focus and respect for everyone's commitment is crucial.

As the head of Fun4walk, it's natural to feel a bit down when a participant left on day one. Shifting the chat focus was a smart move—it keeps us zeroed in on our goals. Don't let this stumble discourage you or the gang. Everyone's on their own fitness ride, and progress takes its own pace for each person. Keep that positive vibe going, cheering each other on, and stick to our initiative's aims. Offer that extra boost to anyone needing it.

I took the lead in prepping a matrix to record our progress—tracking steps, daily highs, and even who's leading the pack so far.

One of our participants really took things up a notch, going beyond expectations with an incredible 48,000-step walk! On average, everyone was walking around 20,000 steps a day. As the challenge rolled on, a bit of friendly competition sparked up, with folks vying to top the step count charts.

Fun4walk stands as a shining example of how a simple idea can inspire folks to boost their fitness and do good for the community. It shows the power of support and motivation that a caring group can provide.

To cap off the challenge, we put our steps to good use by contributing to ANNDAAN (food for all). Everyone pitched in a bit, and we used that collective amount for a food donation at the local temple. It was a satisfying way to wrap up our journey, giving back while improving ourselves.

Participating in a Fun4walk challenge was great. It pushed us to go beyond our usual walking routine and try to break our record each time. Seeing how we all supported and motivated each other was inspiring, making it fun and rewarding with a supportive team. I am a marathon runner, so I initially took it as a kid's play to participate in a walking challenge, but this team completely changed my perception. I had great fun and tried to have a healthy competition walking with this group. Someone rightly said, "If you want to go fast, GO ALONE. If you want to go far, GO TOGETHER."

Thanks, Shiv, for organizing and leading this group. I want to walk together again. - Meenu Mishra

A very nice and motivating experience, especially on 2 days when I completed the last 500 steps by running before 11:59. Looking forward to the next season. - Puneet Maheshwari

A very nice experience. Hope we will have more fun walking. - Shivendu Pathak

CHAPTER TWELVE

A Century Ride to Remember

I've never really liked cycling much. For me, it was just a handy way to get places, not something fun. But my friends loved it. They enjoyed riding their bikes and feeling the breeze on their faces. Next to them, I felt a bit out of place because I didn't share their excitement.

One night, we were all hanging out, and drinking coffee, and as usual, we started talking about cycling. During the chat, one of my friends suggested something big – going on a 100-kilometer bike ride. When I heard this, I felt both nervous and a little excited. It seemed hard, but also kind of exciting.

The discussion about the bike ride was really interesting. We all argued back and forth, each idea better than the last. Finally, we all agreed to do the 100KM ride together. We were half-joking, half-serious, and this decision started a bunch of things I didn't expect.

Then I got ready for the big ride. I didn't cycle much usually, so the idea of riding 100KM felt huge to me. I began with short 10KM rides and slowly worked up to 20KM. I was tired after each ride, but I also felt a little more sure of myself each time.

We picked September for our long ride because the weather would be nice, not too hot or too cold. We planned everything carefully, from the path we'd take to where we'd stop for breaks. But things didn't go as planned. We had to cancel twice because of personal stuff and unexpected problems. This made us all feel pretty sad.

The whole year of 2023 went by, and we never got to do our big 100KM bike ride. It was tough to accept. Every time we had to cancel our plans, it felt like we were losing a dream. We were all disappointed.

But when 2024 started, we felt more determined. We decided that in January 2024, we would finally do our bike ride. It wasn't just about riding a long way anymore. It was about not giving up, sticking together, and showing that we could get past hard times.

Now, as I think about the ride, I'm getting excited again. The big ride is not just about being strong enough to finish. It's also about showing how tough and united we are. This time, we want to make it happen and create a special memory that we'll always remember.